D1606784

Hear No Weevil

Written and Illustrated by
Matt Whitlock

Equipping Kids for Life

COOK COMMUNICATIONS MINISTRIES
Colorado Springs, Colorado • Paris, Ontario
KINGSWAY COMMUNICATIONS LTD
Eastbourne, England

Faith
Parenting
Guide

Ages
4-7

Self-Discipline

A Faith Parenting Guide
can be found starting on page 32

Faith Kidz® is an imprint of
Cook Communications Ministries, Colorado Springs, Colorado 80918
Cook Communications, Paris, Ontario
Kingsway Communications Ltd, Eastbourne, England

HEAR NO WEEVIL
© 2005 by Matt Whitlock

First printing, 2005
Printed in Thailand
2 3 4 5 6 Printing/Year 09 08 07 06 05

Editor: Heather Gemmen
Illustrator: Matt Whitlock
Designer: RJS Design Studio

ISBN: 0781440637

For Shane

Thanks also to:
Chad, Desma, Jason P.,
Jenn, Gil, and Jenny

There's a creepy bug you'd better fear.
He's living deep inside your ear.
A regular liar and constantly evil:
Mr. Fibface—the crusty Boll Weevil.

5

He flits around from ear to ear.
His voice is soft, his message clear:
He'll tell you wrong is sometimes right,
then fly away, far out of sight.

7

But though he's gone, his words remain.

They start to seep into your brain.

Temptations quickly volunteer

and soon the truth is not so clear.

Weevil's coming! He's looking gross!
But he'll find a kid to listen close.
This bug is full of bad advice.
"Being mean is more fun than nice!"

11

He loves the school, so in he zooms.
"Hey listen, Mike! This joint's a tomb!
But you could make the whole class laugh.
Just say that Jill's a big giraffe!"

Weevil jets to the local store
and points out something on the floor.
"Patty! Look! A dollar! Wow!
The lady dropped it! Grab it now!"

14

Jenny is the sweetest thing.
She'd love to have that plastic ring.
A buggy voice makes her eardrum tickle.
"Take it Jenn! It's just a nickel!"

But Jenny's not a silly fool.

She's learned some things in Sunday school.

She knows her thoughts aren't always pure

and prays whenever she's unsure.

When Weevil's words get in her head
She just asks God what to do instead.
"I'd like to keep it, but that'd be wrong.
I'll put it back where it belongs."

Weevil's got that evil grin.
He loves to make the children sin!
If Tim and Sue and Chelsea fall,
Weevil thinks that's best of all!

22

He gears up for a swift attack,
but something stops him in his tracks.
Perhaps these kids have gotten wise
and haven't listened to his lies!

Jenny's gathered all her friends.
She's got advice to recommend.
"You know that bug just can't be trusted.
Sorry Weevil, you've been busted!"

27

"I'm only joking!" Weevil pleads.
"I'd never do those evil deeds!"
But Jenny, Chelsea, Tim, and Sue
send that bug to Timbuktu!

29

So if there's twitching in your ear,
watch out for Weevil buzzing near.
Pray you'll lose that nasty bug
'cause praying makes for good earplugs!

Hear No Weevil

Ages: 4-7

Life Issue: I want my children to avoid temptation and listen for God's advice.

Spiritual Building Block: Self-Discipline (Resisting Temptation)

Do the following activities to help your child understand how to avoid temptation.

 Sight: After reading the story, go back into the book and point to some of Weevil 's earlier whisperings. Ask your child to explain what would have happened if Weevil's advice was followed in each instance. How would it feel to be called a nasty name in front of your class? How would the woman who dropped the dollar feel if someone had taken it off the floor and hadn't looked for it's rightful owner? What if Jenny had stolen the ring and was later caught?

Hear No Weevil

Ages: 4-7

Life Issue: I want my children to avoid temptation and listen for God's advice.

Spiritual Building Block: Self-Discipline (Resisting Temptation)

Do the following activities to help your child understand how to avoid temptation.

Sound: After reading the story, ask your children to share a time in which they were tempted to do something that they shouldn't. Tell them that God can sometimes put good, helpful thoughts in our ears as well, and that we should pray and ask for wisdom to tell the difference between a good 'buzzing sound' and a bad one. Explain that everyone is tempted to do wrong every once in a while—even Jesus! Read Luke 4:1-13 and show how Jesus was able to defeat the devil's 'buzzing.'

Hear No Weevil

Ages: 4-7

Life Issue: I want my children to avoid temptation and listen for God's advice.

Spiritual Building Block: Self-Discipline (Resisting Temptation)

Do the following activities to help your child understand how to avoid temptation.

 Touch: Grab a stuffed animal and pretend it is Evil Weevil. With it, take turns 'buzzing' good and bad suggestions into each other's ears. When Weevil's advice is good, give each other a big hug. When Weevil suggests something bad, shake your head. Read Ephesians 6:10-18, and explain to your child about the putting on the "full armor of God." Grab a pair of earmuffs and use them as your 'armor' while you're each taking turns listening to Weevil.

Add These fun Titles from Matt Whitlock to your Child's Library!

Bionic Butterfly

A Story about Doing Unto Others

Stinky is a slug with a chip on his shoulder who always gives Bill a bad time. Billy's friend, a butterfly who wants to be a superhero, wants to "take Billy down," but Billy's dad has a better idea--the Golden Rule! Through delightful illustrations and hip rhymes, kids learn that "acting" like a strong hero isn't the right approach and that kindness can often win a friend.

ISBN: 0-78144-061-0   ITEM #: 103313   10 x 8   HC   36P

Fleas and Thank You

A Story about Politeness

If kids have to learn about being polite, this is the way to do it! The zany world of artist and author Matt Whitlock comes to life as he boldly exposes the under-appreciated world of fleas and their favorite game show. Even the youngest children will be enchanted as they learn along with Penelope Flea the rewards of politeness.

ISBN: 0-78144-062-9   ITEM #: 103314   10 x 8   HC   36P

Humble Bee

A Story about Pride

Have you learned that your friends don't like your bragging? Humble Bee was a bee who bragged. He made bee-licious snacks that everyone loved--but his boasting created a big problem, and children can learn from his story that everyone should be humble.

ISBN: 0-78143-831-4   ITEM #: 101761   10 x 8   HC   32P

The Non-Praying Mantis

A Story about Prayer and Thankfulness

Have you ever asked God for something but didn't get it? After a big disappointment, the Non-Praying Mantis finally discovers the secret od seeing her prayers answered. Children will learn the valuable lesson that, even when they don't get the answer they want, it's important to talk to God.

ISBN: 0-78143-830-6   ITEM #: 101762   10 x 8   HC   32P

The GigANTic Little Hero

A Story about Perseverance

An ant who lacks confidence seeks the aid of a spider and a grasshopper to carry a heavy load. When they suddenly leave him, he's unaware that he's carrying the weight all alone! He learns he CAN do the job which builds his confidence and courage, and through his story, children will see that they too can have the confidence to do any task!

ISBN: 0-78143-517-X   ITEM #: 99929   10 x 8   HC   32P

Order Your Copies Today!

Order Online: www.cookministries.com, Phone: 1-800-323-7543, Or Visit your Local Christian Bookstore

The Word at Work Around the World

What would you do if you wanted to share God's love with children on the streets of your city? That's the dilemma David C. Cook faced in 1870's Chicago. His answer was to create literature that would capture children's hearts.

Out of those humble beginnings grew a worldwide ministry that has used literature to proclaim God's love and disciple generation after generation. Cook Communications Ministries is committed to personal discipleship—to helping people of all ages learn God's Word, embrace his salvation, walk in his ways, and minister in his name.

Faith Kidz, RiverOak, Honor, Life Journey, Victor, NextGen . . . every time you purchase a book produced by Cook Communications Ministries, you not only meet a vital personal need in your life or in the life of someone you love, but you're also a part of ministering to José in Colombia, Humberto in Chile, Gousa in India, or Lidiane in Brazil. You help make it possible for a pastor in China, a child in Peru, or a mother in West Africa to enjoy a life-changing book. And because you helped, children and adults around the world are learning God's Word and walking in his ways.

Thank you for your partnership in helping to disciple the world. May God bless you with the power of his Word in your life.

For more information about our international ministries,
visit www.ccmi.org.